Taking Care of a Bird

Elsie Nelley
Photographs by Lindsay Edwards

Contents

Goal

To take care of a pet bird

Materials

Every Day

You will need:

- clean paper

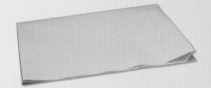

- birdseed

- cold water

- little bits of apple

Every Week

You will need these things, too:

- a small box

- warm water
  in a big bowl

- an old, clean towel

Wash your hands
before and **after**
you feed the bird
and clean the cage.

Steps

Every Day

1. Open the cage door. Do not let the bird fly out.

2. Take out any food the bird has not eaten.

3. Close the cage door.

4. Pull out the **plastic tray**.

5. Put clean paper
   on the tray
   and push it back
   into the cage.

6. Take out the **food dish** and fill it with new seeds.

7. Put the dish back
inside the cage.

8. Take out the **water dish**.

9. Wash it and fill it with clean water.

10. Put the dish back inside the cage.

11. Open the cage door.

12. Put some bits of apple on the tray.

13. Close the cage door.

Steps

Every Week

1. Ask Mom to take the bird out of the cage.

   Put the bird
   in a small box.
   It will be safe
   inside the box.

2. Clean all the things inside the cage.

3. Wash the inside and outside of the cage.

4. Let the cage dry.

5. Put clean paper
   on the plastic tray.

6. Put some bits of apple
   on the tray.

7. Fill the food dish
   and the water dish again.

8. Put the bird back
in the cage.

Glossary

food dish

plastic tray

water dish